# ★ BETTE DAVIS ★
## A TRIBUTE 1908~1989

## · ROGER · BAKER ·

GALLERY BOOKS
An Imprint of W. H. Smith Publishers Inc.
112 Madison Avenue
New York City 10016

"No-one faintly like an actress got off the train ...." Bette Davis was a very ordinary-looking girl when she arrived in Hollywood in 1931. She wanted to be an actress, not a glamor girl!

In none of the eighty-plus films she made in a career lasting from 1931 to 1989 did Bette Davis make any concessions to an image. And yet an image emerged (previous page): the mouth devouring rather than sensual, the lipstick riding over the natural curve of the upper lip; the hair with its knife-edge parting, yet ready to be tossed back in anger or passion; the heavy eyebrows; the threatening smile ... never a woman to be trifled with.

CLB 2547
© 1989 Colour Library Books Ltd, Godalming, Surrey, England.
This edition published in 1989 by Gallery Books, an imprint of W.H. Smith, Inc,
112 Madison Avenue, New York 10016.
Printed and bound in Italy by New Interlitho
All rights reserved
ISBN 0 8317 0800 X
Gallery Books are available for bulk purchase for sales promotions and premium use. For details write or telephone the Manager of Special Sales, W.H. Smith, Publishers, Inc.,
112 Madison Avenue, New York, New York 10016. (212) 532-6600.

PHOTO CREDITS
The Ronald Grant Collection: pages 5, 11, 13, 15, 18, 20, 21, 22 (bottom),25 (top left and bottom), 26 (top), 27, 36 (bottom left), 48 (bottom), 62
The Joel Finler Collection pages: 2, 7, 9, 16, 17,19, 23, 24, 25 (top right), 26 (bottom), 28, 29, 32, 33, 37, 38, 39, 41, 45 (top left), 49, 54 (top), 55, 57, 60, 61
Syndication International Ltd: pages 11, 10, 4, 45 (bottom)
The Hulton Collection: pages 22 (top), 30, 31, 34, 35, 36 (top, and bottom right), 40, 42, 43,44,45 (top right), 46, 47, 48 (top), 50, 51, 52, 53, 54 (bottom), 56, 58, 59, 63, 64

★ *Bette Davis* ★

For more than twenty years Bette Davis was the undisputed First Lady of the Screen. When she died at the age of 81 on October 7, 1989 tributes were extensive, yet only an older generation of film-goers would have had any clear idea of her true stature as one of Hollywood's most assertive and powerful actresses. And in any assessment of Bette Davis's work, the word "actress" is important and must be used with precision.

For this was, perhaps, the most important quality, among many others, that separated her and her work from that of the other stars Hollywood was busy molding and turning out during the heyday of the studios in the 1930s and 1940s. Female stars were expected at least to be decorative, like Dorothy Lamour, and preferably glamorous and full of allure, like Garbo. They were also expected to be sympathetic and have a certain warmth, whether this was projected through Merle Oberon-style high passion, or the girl-next-door quality of Janet Gaynor. And whatever role these stars tackled, their intrinsic qualities were always allowed to show through.

This was not the Davis style. Glamor was not a commodity she dealt in. She faced the stills camera with a beady, challenging stare – no crossed legs, turn of the shoulder or inviting smile. The gallery of roles she undertook, from that in her first movie in 1931 through to her final screen appearance in *The Whales of August* in 1988, is an alarming lineup of calculating, fighting, determined women. She took each script (and many were derisory) by the scruff of the neck and shook it until her own role emerged, and she would immerse herself in this without compromise. Slut or grande dame, waitress or drunk, queen or bitch, she made no concessions to being "nice" or being "pretty." Nor was she ever frightened of being vulgar.

From Davis audiences expected – and got – high drama and, in the series of films she made at the height of her career, the spectacle of a ruthless woman clawing her way to some goal. One commentator has suggested that she was the first great incarnation of the castrating female (even before this phrase was known or understood). Even in comedy she had a way of delivering her lines, a certain manner that suggested this was no girl to be trifled with. As a result, her appeal during the '30s and '40s was probably mainly with female audiences. Davis did things and went places like no other star, and certainly not like her audiences. But she did it for them. For a whole generation of women, she acted out their subconscious dreams of revenge and their aspirations to glory.

Inevitably, she began to dominate the films she appeared in, and it is sometimes difficult to remember who her co-stars were. Although she worked with many of Hollywood's leading actors, she always seemed to reduce them to shadowy figures – Claude Rains was one of the few who held his own; female co-stars were efficiently dealt with, too. In one of her best films, *All About Eve* (1950) she was given a high-class lineup of co-stars including George Sanders, Gary Merrill, Anne Baxter, Celeste Holm and the then relatively-unknown Marilyn Monroe. It is still regarded as containing the wittiest and most literate script of any film, and it won an Oscar for writer-director Joseph L. Mankiewicz. But the enduring memories, effacing all others, are of Davis rapping out the memorable lines, posing, snapping, dragging on her cigarette, flashing her headlamp eyes, and generally creating a storm.

She won the New York Critics' Award for her performance in this film. And this performance is a compendium of all the mannerisms and tricks that she had been acquiring. Although it was often said that Davis was "inimitable," she has, over the years, become the target of parodists and satirists who mainly targeted her crisp delivery of lines and somewhat angular, jerky movements of shoulder and elbow. But this is superficial, cartoon-like; the essential qualities she brought to the screen truly were inimitable. The intensity – one critic called it "electric" – and the mannerisms were there from the beginning, and they simply became more emphatic over the years. But the sheer variety of her roles and, in her great years, consistent critical acclaim prove that she could create interpretations which transcended, and often obliterated, her external tics.

Audiences are unwilling to submit to a repetition of the same performance year after year: a cigarette held shoulder-high, a dramatic exit are trademarks – not the material itself. She was nominated for an Oscar ten times, and won it twice – for *Dangerous* (1935) and *Jezebel* (1938); the first is almost completely forgotten now, the second is seen occasionally and is regarded as a vintage Davis performance.

"If Hollywood didn't work out I was all prepared to be the best secretary in the world." This comment from Bette Davis may have raised a laugh at some press conference or other, but it is clear that her destiny was to be an actress.

She was born Ruth Elizabeth Davis in Lowell, Massachusetts, in 1908, and it was when she was at school that she decided she wanted to go on the stage. So she went on to study at the John Murray Anderson school and from there joined a summer-stock company in Rochester, which was directed by George Cukor. Today, Cukor is remembered as one of Hollywood's most elegant and stylish directors, with a special flair for showcasing his female stars – *A Star is Born* and *The Women* are among his more enduring creations. Back in the early '20s his eye for style was already in focus and the stock company included young players like Miriam Hopkins and Robert Montgomery. However, he simply could not get on with the pushy Miss Davis and fired her. She got a job with the Provincetown Players and toured in Ibsen and Chekhov among others. But her eyes were on Hollywood and she went for a screen test at the Goldwyn Studios, which she failed. "When I saw my first screen test I ran from the projection room screaming" she is reported to have said later.

Undeterred, she had another go, this time with Universal, and she passed. The studio boss, Carl Laemmle, had a small role in mind for her, but when he met her he commented: "She has as much sex appeal as Slim Somerville ... I can't imagine any guy giving her a tumble."

Many young actresses might have found this kind of reaction depressing. There is an anecdote that a studio worker, sent to meet Davis off the train when she first arrived in Hollywood, returned alone saying: "No-one faintly like an actress got off the train." And it is likely that she quickly realised that she wouldn't slip easily into a world so dominated by glamor. But with the guts and determination that characterized her whole career, she decided that now she was there she was going to become, and presumably look like, an actress.

Her first film was *Bad Sister* (1931), in which she played the good sister and went unnoticed by press and public. But she was on contract and fielded every film the studio threw at her. During that first year she appeared in four films, ranging from drama to comedy to mystery. She dyed her hair blonde and was cast opposite George Arliss in *The Man Who Played God* (1932). Whether it was the hair or the prestige of playing opposite one of Hollywood's most noted actors, is not clear, but she now began to get noticed, and in 1932 made no less than eleven films, appearing with stars like Barbara Stanwyck, Ruth Chatterton, Spencer Tracey and Douglas Fairbanks, Jr.

---

Hollywood soon got to work on the young Bette Davis; make-up artists and the stills cameramen groomed the child into something approaching contemporary standards of glamor.

She had now been taken up by the Warner Brothers studio, where Warner himself noted that she had a "magic quality that transformed this bland and not beautiful little girl into a great artist when she was playing bitchy roles." Even so, 1933 gave her little to do – a thriller, a musical in which she didn't sing or dance and *Ex Lady*, which she was to describe as "a piece of junk. My shame was only exceeded by my fury."

The turning point in her career came in 1934 when the director John Cromwell wanted to borrow her for a film version of Somerset Maugham's story *Of Human Bondage*, which he was making for RKO. Warners were unwilling, but Davis, starting to show fire, fought for the role and eventually secured it. It made her a star. She probably realized that the part of Mildred – a vicious, grasping waitress who enslaves and ruins a young doctor (Leslie Howard) – would give her the opportunity she had been waiting for. Critical acclaim was wide and unanimous; there was surprise that she wasn't nominated for an Oscar, and Warners were, of course, thrilled at this reaction.

But she flatly refused to do the next film they offered her (something umpromisingly called *The Case of the Howling Dog*), and her attitude was strengthened by the success of the Maugham film and by more excellent notices for *Housewife* (1934). What she wanted to do was play Elizabeth I in *Mary of Scotland,* but failed to get the part (she was, of course, to play Elizabeth twice, later on in her career). A series of uninteresting films followed, but at least she was now starred.

But then came *Dangerous* (1935), in which she played a once-great actress who has drunk herself into the gutter and is rescued by a young architect, Franchot Tone. Although soapy and sentimental, it produced a powerful performance from Davis, and she won her first Oscar for it. Her next film was also a winner – *The Petrified Forest*. "She does not have to be hysterical to be credited with a grand portrayal" said one critic. The film was also important to the careers of co-stars Humphrey Bogart and Leslie Howard.

Despite these splendid examples of her talent, Warners continued to cast her in dreary films which she made the best of even when they were trivial and unrewarding. However, the crunch came when they offered her something called *God's Country and the Woman* which, again, she flatly refused to do. As a result, Warners suspended her and took her off their payroll ($5,000 a week). Davis promptly set sail for England, where she had been offered two films, with script approval, to be made in Italy and France. However, Warners issued an injunction for breach of contract, and Davis in turn filed suit, and lost. Her contract bound her to Warner Brothers until 1942.

This was a significant episode, since Davis's stand was one of the first times that a star had rebelled against the studio contract system – just as Marilyn Monroe was to do twenty years later. The public, of course, saw this off-stage drama as a typical Davis scenario, and her reputation for being difficult and feisty off screen as well as on became established.

And, as in so many of her films, she won a kind of victory in the end, for Warners graciously paid her share of the damages, and on her return accorded her the deference due to such a box-office draw and, more importantly, began to prepare better scripts for her. The construction of the "Bette Davis vehicle" had begun.

First came two gangster movies – *Marked Woman* and *Kid Galahad*, and then a comedy – *It's Love I'm After* – with Leslie Howard and *That Certain Woman* with Henry Fonda, which prompted the magazine *Photoplay* to observe that the star exerted "every ounce of her undeniable ability to turn sheer melodrama into legitimate emotion." Then in 1938 came *Jezebel*, for which she won her second Oscar.

This film was tailor-made for her. It has been suggested that she was offered the role in consolation for not being cast in *Gone With the Wind*, and the films do have strong similarities. Davis plays a viciously calculating Southern belle, shocking the decorum of local

society. Her co-stars were Henry Fonda and George Brent. She got rave reviews and was described as "one of the wonders of Hollywood."

The wonder continued to assert herself, and once again was suspended for refusing two scripts. However, she consented to *The Sisters* with Errol Flynn, and leaped at what is now regarded as a Davis classic – *Dark Victory*, a tragic melodrama about a spoiled society girl going blind. This authentic tear-jerker won her a Picturegoer Gold Medal. She made an impression in *Juarez* (1939) and even more so in *The Old Maid*, in which she and her sister (Miriam Hopkins) fight for the love of a child. "Perhaps Miss Davis is a great actress ..." mused novelist Graham Greene. Then came another classic – *The Private Lives of Elizabeth and Essex* – her first film in color and with Errol Flynn. She dominated the film and fixed for a generation an image of what Elizabeth I was "really like." The role demanded – and got – discipline, as well as a crisp, dry delivery, of which she was a mistress. By now Bette Davis had supplanted Shirley Temple as America's favorite star, and in 1940 was voted Queen of Hollywood.

By 1938 she could be pretty if she wanted to, if it was relevant to her role. In *Jezebel* (above left) it certainly was.

Elizabeth I of England was a role she longed to play, and eventually she played it twice. Her face was the wrong shape, but the mouth and the eyes carried the day (above right).

Everything was going for her now, and a succession of first-rate films followed. There was *All This and Heaven Too* with Charles Boyer, *The Letter,* of which the noted film critic Pauline Kael said that Davis gave "what is very likely the best study of female sexual hypocrisy in film history," *The Great Lie* with Mary Astor, but then a bit of drivel with James Cagney called *The Bride Came C.O.D.*.

In 1941 yet another Davis classic was being filmed – a version of Lillian Hellman's gripping melodrama about double-dealing and murder within a Southern family presided over by chief vixen Regina (Davis). She was powerful, intimidating, unscrupulous, and gave what is still

regarded as one of her very finest performances. She showed a sure flair for comedy in *The Man Who Came to Dinner,* and returned to being a mega-bitch in *This Our Life* (1942). A wonderful weepie followed – *Now Voyager* – in which Miss Davis transformed herself from a dreary frump into a glamorous, cigarette-smoking woman of the world. This is the film that includes one of the most famous of all concluding lines as Davis, melting into Paul Henreid's arms for the final fade, murmurs: "Oh Gerry – don't let's ask for the moon – we have the stars." Picturegoer awarded her another Gold Medal.

In 1943 she delighted her fans by participating in the all-star morale-booster *Thank Your Lucky Stars* when she croaked her way through a song "They're Either Too Young or Too Old." A film version of Lillian Hellman's play *Watch on the Rhine* followed, and *Old Acquaintance,* in which Davis plays the author of serious novels who loses the man she loves to Miriam Hopkins, who has made a fortune from trashy "best-sellers."

*Mr. Skeffington,* in which she played a selfish woman whose beauty is fading, teamed Bette Davis with the formidable Claude Rains. She marries him, divorces him and then welcomes him back when he is blind and cannot see that she has lost her looks. They don't make films like that these days! Nor do they make films like *The Corn is Green* (1945), based on Emlyn Williams' quite serious and thoughtful play about a village schoolmistress bent on guiding a poor kid into higher education.

In fact the Davis star seemed to be on the decline. Her next five films were derisory and trivial, and she asked to be released from her contract with Warner Brothers; the request was granted. In 1948 she had been the highest paid star of all time.

Naturally, there was no shortage of film offers, and she accepted a meaty part in a divorce drama for RKO called *Payment on Demand,* but this was not released until the film she was doing for 20th Century Fox had been seen. This was *All About Eve*, arguably the best thing she ever did, the bitchy backstage story of a star toppled from her pedestal by a wily young actress played by Anne Baxter. This success put her back in the headlines, but rather than opening up a new phase in her career the film seems, in retrospect, to have marked the end of her supremacy.

Other films followed during the 1950s, but they provoked one commentator to remark: "Only bad films are good enough for her." Perhaps the only worthwhile effort during this period was *The Virgin Queen,* in which she recreated the role of Elizabeth I with dialogue, which was a convincing pastiche of the style of Elizabeth's letters and speeches. It was a flashy and flamboyant performance that demolished the contributions of Richard Todd and Joan Collins.

Once more it seemed as though her fortunes were on the wane. She did a cameo as Catherine the Great in *John Paul Jones* (1959) and after the flop of *A Pocketful of Miracles* she took full page advertisements in the trade press asking for work. What she got was, it turned out, another blockbuster – Robert Aldrich's Gothic chiller *Whatever Happened to Baby Jane?,* in which she was starred opposite her long-term rival in the Hollywood drama stakes, Joan Crawford. They played two grotesque, reclusive sisters living in a crumbling mansion. Davis is a faded former child movie star who gets her kicks by mentally torturing her crippled sister. Both actresses went completely over the top to the delight of audiences then and ever since.

In 1964 she played twins in a minor thriller *Dead Ringer,* and the following year came the follow-up to *Baby Jane,* in which she was this time teamed with Olivia de Havilland, who agreed to the role as a favor to Davis, a long-time friend. It is a macabre piece of horror, again

---

Relaxing on the set, the characters she was playing disappeared, and
the camera caught a young actress having a coffee and a cigarette
between rehearsals.

directed by Aldrich, and considered superior to its predecessor. British critic Kenneth Tynan commented on Bette Davis's ability to "squeeze genuine pathos from a role conceived in cardboard."

Her final phase of film-making was in England, where she worked for Hammer, the company that specialized in horror movies. *The Nanny* (1965) gave her a substantial role which she played with great fidelity, and *Connecting Rooms* (1970) with Michael Redgrave was acceptable. In between, however, came *The Anniversary* (1967), the film version of a play which had amused London a few years earlier, about a horrendous mother who uses devious and cruel tricks to dominate her adult children. Davis, in baroque makeup and with black eye-patch, could not prevent this from being one of the most awful films ever made.

As she grew older, a certain softness developed, and in some roles she was able to lend middle-age a gentle dignity.

However, high drama was never far away. In *The Anniversary* (facing page) she acted up a storm with only one eye to help her, though many critics consider this her worst film.

Although there were only sporadic films until *The Whales of August* (1988), in which she was paired with the 92-year-old Lillian Gish, Bette Davis remained a vivid figure in the film world, appearing at Oscar ceremonies, attending festivals, delivering lectures and lending her authority to juries and television shows.

It is part of a star's charisma that audiences grow to imagine that their private life and behavior somehow resembles the roles they play on screen. Bette Davis's private life never made the kind of headlines achieved by some of her contemporaries, but over the years her reputation as a difficult, self-willed woman grew. Her confrontation with the studios, frequent rows with directors and co-stars, an unwillingness to suffer fools gladly, and a sharp tongue tended to keep people at arm's length. "Surely no-one but a mother could have loved Bette Davis at the height of her career," remarked Brian Aherne. She married four times: Harmon Nelson (1932-38), Arthur Farnsworth (1941-43), William Grant Sherry – by whom she had a daughter – (1945), and actor Gary Merrill (1950-60). When asked if she would contemplate marrying for a fifth time, she replied: "If I found a man who had $15 million, would sign over half of it to me before the marriage, and guarantee he'd be dead within a year ...."

Thousands of words have been spent trying to sum up the special stature and charisma of Bette Davis. Perhaps the best attempt is to be found in a conversation that the critic Kenneth Tynan had with another Hollywood great, Katharine Hepburn, in 1952.

"'Cagney and Bogart and Tracy and Bette Davis – they're all *invulnerable*, is that the word I mean ?' I said it was. She found in them a certainty, a diamond core which could not be dimmed or devalued: they were stars."

## THE FILMS OF BETTE DAVIS

| | | |
|---|---|---|
| *Bad Sister* 1931 | *Secret Agent* 1935 | *Deception* 1946 |
| *Seed* 1931 | *The Petrified Forest* 1936 | *Winter Meeting* 1948 |
| *Waterloo Bridge* 1931 | *Golden Arrow* 1936 | *June Bride* 1948 |
| *Way Back Home* 1931 | *Satan Met a Lady* 1936 | *Beyond the Forest* 1949 |
| *The Menace* 1932 | *Marked Woman* 1936 | *All About Eve* 1950 |
| *Hell's House* 1932 | *Kid Gallahad* 1937 | *Payment on Demand* 1951 |
| *The Man who Played God* 1932 | *It's Love I'm After* 1937 | *Another Man's Poison* 1951 |
| *So Big* 1932 | *That Certain Woman* 1937 | *Phone Call From a Stranger* 1952 |
| *The Rich are Always with Us* 1932 | *Jezebel* 1938 | *The Star* 1952 |
| *The Dark Horse* 1932 | *The Sisters* 1938 | *The Virgin Queen* 1955 |
| *Cabin in the Cotton* 1932 | *Dark Victory* 1939 | *Storm Santa* 1956 |
| *20,000 Years in Sing Sing* 1932 | *Juarez* 1939 | *The Wedding Breakfast* 1956 |
| *Three on a Match* 1932 | *The Old Maid* 1939 | *The Scapegoat* 1959 |
| *Parachute Jumper* 1932 | *Elizabeth and Essex* 1939 | *John Paul Jones* 1959 |
| *The Working Man* 1932 | *All this and Heaven Too* 1940 | *A Pocketful of Miracles* 1961 |
| *Ex Lady* 1933 | *The Letter* 1940 | *Whatever Happened to Baby Jane* 1962 |
| *Bureau of Missing Persons* 1933 | *The Great Lie* 1941 | *Where Love Has Gone* 1964 |
| *Fashions* 1934 | *The Bride Came COD* 1941 | *The Empty Canvas* 1964 |
| *The Big Shakedown* 1934 | *The Little Foxes* 1941 | *Hush Hush Sweet Charlotte* 1964 |
| *Jimmy the Gent* 1934 | *The Man Who Came to Dinner* 1941 | *The Nanny* 1965 |
| *Fog over Frisco* 1934 | *In this Our Life* 1942 | *The Anniversary* 1967 |
| *Of Human Bondage* 1934 | *Now, Voyager* 1942 | *Connecting Rooms* 1969 |
| *Housewife* 1934 | *Watch on the Rhine* 1943 | *Bunny O'Hare* 1971 |
| *Bordertown* 1934 | *Old Acquaintance* 1943 | *Death on the Nile* 1978 |
| *The Girl from Tenth Avenue* 1934 | *Thank Your Lucky Stars* 1943 | *Watcher in the Woods* 1980 |
| *Dangerous* 1935 | *Mr. Skeffington* 1944 | *The Whales of August* 1988 |
| *Front Page Woman* 1935 | *The Corn is Green* 1945 | |
| | *Stolen Life* 1946 | |

In old age she could still capitalize on her powerful looks and decades of dramatic experience to create unforgettable cameo performances, such as that in *Madame Sin*.

# ★ Bette Davis ★
## · A LIFE IN PICTURES ·

She was born Ruth Elizabeth Davis in Lowell, Massachusetts in 1908. The Bette came from Balzac somewhat later.

Trying to be pretty (overleaf top left) did not become her, and the curled hair, the winsome smile and the mousy little-girl look won her few friends during her early Hollywood days. But the mouse learnt fast; the mouth began to take on the shape it would hold for the rest of her life, and the hair to look under control (facing page).

After a year in Hollywood, and four unremarkable films, she dyed her hair blonde for *The Menace* and a new image was under way (facing page).

The blonde hair, the clearer make-up – especially that distinctive mouth (above left) – were beginning to work for her. In 1932 she made eleven films. One may wonder how the seriously ambitious actress felt about posing for routine "glamor" stills (above right).

When her original studio, Universal, dropped her, Bette was taken up by Warner Brothers, for whom she worked – with a few hiccups – for the next ten years.

*Cabin in the Cotton* (facing page top) was a significant film in her career. It was her first wickedly sexy role, spent trying to tempt Richard Barthelmess away from virtue. Michael Curtiz directed.

"Probably the best performance ever recorded on screen by a US actress" was one verdict on *Of Human Bondage (facing page bottom)*, in which Bette played the vicious waitress who lays waste Leslie Howard's life. It was a role she fought for.

The slightly tight smile might suggest that she was none too sure of
the furry creature on her lap, but Hollywood was clearly grooming a
sophisticated young woman by now.

*Front Page Woman* (1935) (right) was one of a rapid sequence of
films Warner Brothers threw her into and in which she was now
starred, but which made no particular impact on the press
or the public.

In *Dangerous* (1935) she played a hard-drinking, self-destructive actress who gives up her true love, Franchot Tone, for her crippled husband. "Mawkish and trashy" was one verdict, but it won Davis her first Academy Award and was the first film to make her audiences take a stand – love her, or loathe her.

Facing page top: contract signing, surrounded by Hollywood moguls with relieved smiles. In 1936, dissatisfied with the material she was being given, Davis was suspended. Litigation followed, but all ended well when she commited herself to Warner Brothers until 1942. By 1937, Davis was being given films she could make a meal of. *Marked Woman* (facing page bottom) was a melodrama based on the career of Lucky Luciano in which she played a smart young clip-joint hostess who turns police informer. Her performance was vibrant. Humphrey Bogart played the prosecutor.

The star was maturing; the blonde hair was forgotten, and while she
was playing gangsters' molls, the studio stills man tried to give her a
sultry, glamorous look (facing page and below left). This didn't last.

Bette Davis won her second Oscar for her performance in *Jezebel*
(1938) (top right and above), in which she played an unscrupulous
and manipulating Southern belle. Henry Fonda and George Brent
were the men in her life, and Fay Bainter won a
Best Supporting Actress award.

A FIRST NATIONAL PICTURE

BETTE DAVIS : DARK VICTORY :

By the late 1930s, Bette Davis was starring in a series of made-to-measure vehicles for most of which she is best remembered today. Through these her final image emerged – the simple hair, the angular elbows and shoulders, the ever-present cigarette – and a challenging look.

*Dark Victory* (1939) (facing page top) is a classic vehicle. Davis plays a rich, spoiled girl doomed by a fatal disease who throws herself into a spiral of meaningless pleasures. She is, however, redeemed by the love of her doctor, George Brent. Humphrey Bogart and Ronald Reagan also feature.

Davis did not always go over the top – she could be subdued and self-effacing, as in the serious-minded 1943 movie of Lillian Hellman's war-time *Watch on the Rhine* (facing page bottom), in which she starred with Paul Lukas, who won an Academy Award for the film.

Bette Davis realized her long-standing wish to play Elizabeth I in
1939 with *The Private Lives of Elizabeth and Essex* (facing page) –
her first color film. It was a magnetic, tough performance and
completely overshadowed the inept Essex of Errol Flynn.

Her Regina in *The Little Foxes* (above) created a sensation. "Bette
Davis has never given a finer performance ..." wrote one critic. The
film became one of the top money-earners of 1941.

Bette Davis married four times. Her third marriage, in 1945, was to William Grant Sherry, and they honeymooned (this page) in White Mountains, Littleton, New Hampshire. The sight of the sophisticated Davis enjoying a casual picnic delighted her public. This marriage produced her only child, a daughter. Facing page: mother and daughter at the Cannes Film Festival in 1963.

Left: lighting and camera tests for *The Corn is Green* (1945). Davis was only thirty-six when she was cast as Miss Moffat, the ageing spinster schoolteacher of Emlyn Williams' play, and seemed to lack the wisdom and solidity required. But, as a between-takes shot (above) suggests, she did her best to project warmth and sympathy.

Although tough and with a reputation for being difficult, Bette Davis
was a ranking member of the Hollywood aristocracy and made
regular appearances at studio functions, both personal, such as the
christening of Hedy Lamarr's daughter (facing page bottom) and
official, such as a Hollywood Press Association cocktail party (facing
page top). Above: chatting to Hollywood's influential gossip
writer Hedda Hopper.

During the Second World War the Hollywood stars, including Bette Davis, got together to create a servicemen's rendezvous. Here, on-leave forces could chat with the stars. Davis put in a brief appearance in a morale-boosting film, *Hollywood Canteen*, which was based on the establishment.

Claude Rains was one of the few Hollywood leading men who were able to hold their own when co-starred with Bette Davis. They made several films together, including the delightful costume drama *Mr. Skeffington*, and *Deception* (above left).

In *Deception* (facing page bottom right), Claude Rains played the
greatest composer in the United States, with Davis as his mistress.
She resorts to firearms to escape him, because she really loves a
cellist, played by Paul Henreid. Despite overcrowded studio
conditions (above), their scenes together are convincing enough.

"Surely no one but a mother could have loved Bette Davis at the height of her career ..." commented her once-co-star Brian Aherne.

In 1950, just when it seemed her career had peaked and was on the decline, Bette Davis was offered the role of the ageing star Margo Channing in *All About Eve (left)*, which arguably produced her finest ever performance. The all-star line-up included George Sanders and the young Marilyn Monroe in one of her best early roles.

"Nobody knew what I looked like because I never looked the same way twice" Bette Davis once remarked. She was referring to her film roles, but, as these informal snaps taken at receptions (above and overleaf left), on film sets (facing page and overleaf right bottom) and at a Hollywood tribute to studio head Jack Warner (overleaf right top) suggest, her real-life image could change considerably too.

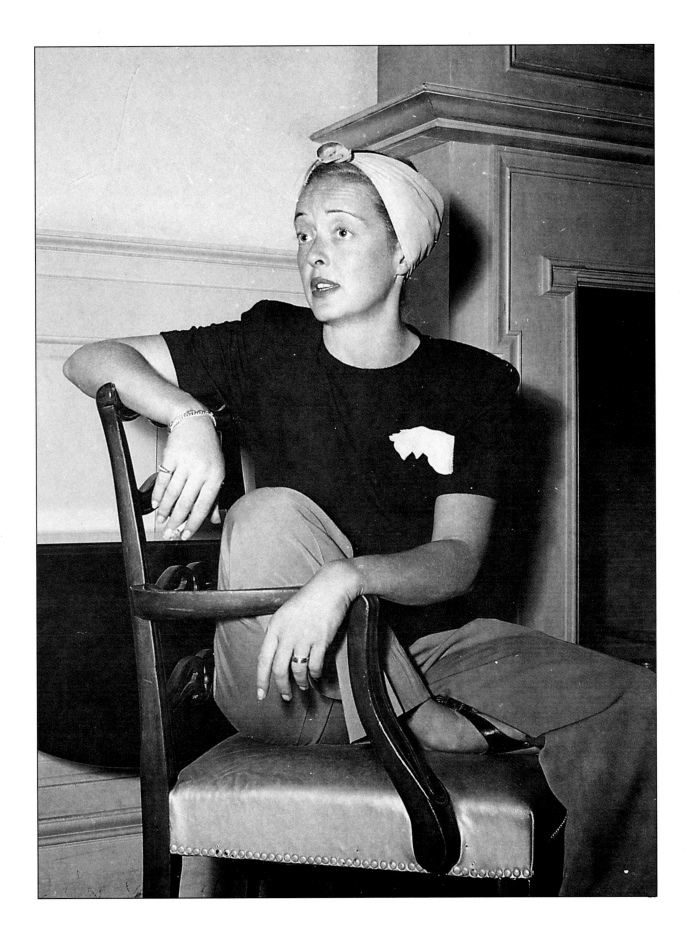

Bette Davis started her career as a stage actress, but did not return to
the live theatre until the early '50s, when she accepted a small role in
Tennessee Williams' play *The Night of the Iguana*. Much more to
the taste – and delight – of her fans, however, was a revue, *Two's
Company (above)*, in which she sang, danced and laid about her in a
series of satirical sketches.

"Only bad films are good enough for her," wrote one critic when
*The Star* (facing page bottom) appeared in 1953. Sterling Hayden is
the man who saves the once successful but now ageing star from her
downward spiral into drink.

While making *The Virgin Queen*, Davis's appearances at Hollywood
parties (facing page top right) seemed to reflect her current role.

Davis had her second chance to play Elizabeth I in a film intended to focus on Sir Walter Raleigh. She asked for the role, got it, and the film was finally called *The Virgin Queen* (1955) (below left). She tackled it full steam ahead, but it was never a success.

By the late 1950s Bette Davis was looking outside America for suitable movies. In 1958 she went to Italy to make a bio-pic – *John Paul Jones*, in which she played Catherine the Great. Her appearance was too late to save the movie. Much of the picture was filmed aboard the *Bonhomme Richard* (these pages).

She returned to films in 1961 with *A Pocketful of Miracles (these pages)*, in which she played Apple Annie, a street vendor who becomes a lady for a day to impress her daughter. Glenn Ford, who also starred, had specifically asked for Davis, but the venture was not a success.

During the next few years she traveled around from film to film,
always arriving with energy and a feeling of optimism: at Los
Angeles airport (facing page top right), in Rome (facing page: top left
and bottom left), in Perth (overleaf right top) and in her suite at
London's Savoy Hotel (above).

In 1962 Davis had been a hit in the macabre essay *Whatever Happened to Baby Jane*. In that film she played alongside Joan Crawford. In its successor, *Hush Hush Sweet Charlotte*, her long-term friend Olivia de Havilland agreed to co-star, with great success. They are seen here in an informal moment together.

In 1963 she arrived in Rome (previous pages left bottom right and above) to make *The Empty Canvas*, in which she overacts as a wildly possessive mother. She described making it as "a nightmare," which is what audiences felt watching it. Horst Buchholtz is the son, Catherine Spaak the girl he fancies.

Nineteen-sixty-five found Bette Davis in England, working mainly for Hammer, a studio specializing in routine horror movies. *The Nanny* (below and bottom) had great potential as a thriller, with Davis as a dowdy, repressed nanny whose charge suspects her of having murdered his little sister. However, her starry acting jarred with the more restrained style of the rest of the cast.

*The Anniversary* (1967) (right) revealed Davis as a grotesque mother resorting to every kind of unpleasant trick to prevent her family gaining independence. It worked as a kind of Grand Guignol on stage, but the movie was repellent. Jack Hedley and Sheila Hancock also featured.

Of the films Bette Davis made in England at this time, *Connecting Rooms* (below and facing page top) is considered the best of a pretty poor lot. In it she portrayed an elderly busker who plays the 'cello in London's theaterland and forms a relationship with a disgraced headmaster, played by Michael Redgrave. Alexis Kanner also featured.

Even more embarrassing for Bette Davis fans was a 1971 epic called
*Bunny O'Hare*, in which she and Ernest Borgnine play a couple of
elderly bank robbers who disguise themselves as hippies and make
their getaway by motorbike.

Above: at a press reception held in October 1975 at the London
Palladium to launch her one-woman show (top and facing page),
which she presented in several leading theaters in England. In it she
answered questions from the audience and offered a few Hollywood
anecdotes and reminiscences of her past.

In 1978 Bette Davis lent her weight to the all-star production of
Agatha Christie's *Death on the Nile*. Others in the cast included
David Niven, Peter Ustinov (facing page bottom) as the detective
Hercule Poirot, and Maggie Smith (previous page right), who scored
a huge hit as Davis's eccentric nurse-companion.

*Watcher in the Woods* (1980) (below and overleaf top) was an attempt by Walt Disney Studios to make more adult films. They came up with a genuinely spooky story about a young girl and a ghost, filmed in beautiful English locations. Lynn Holly Johnson was the girl and Bette Davis was memorable.

Bette Davis blows out the candles on her birthday cake at a party
during the filming of *Watcher in the Woods*.